1/07

How Did That Get Here?

The Biography of Coffee

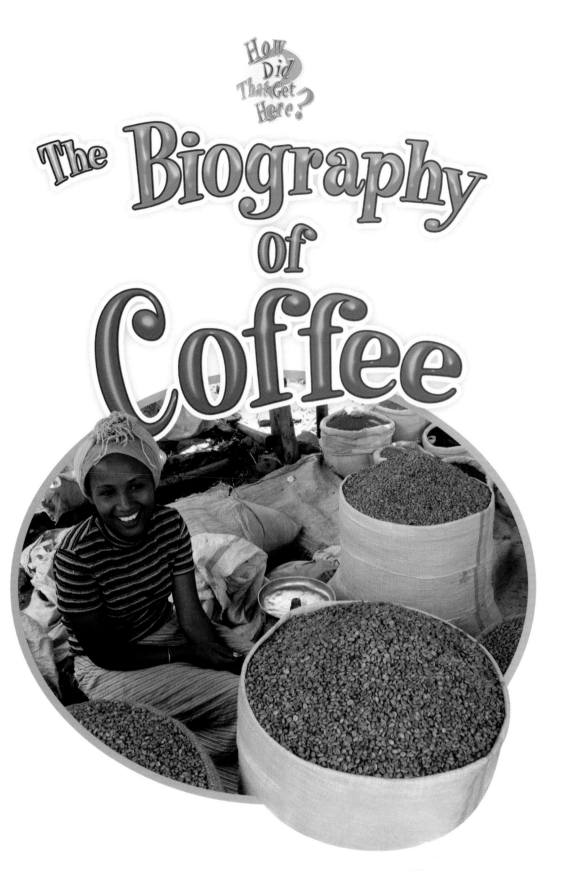

Adrianna Morganelli

 Crabtree Publishing Company
www.crabtreebooks.com

Crabtree Publishing Company

www.crabtreebooks.com

For Josie and Charlene, and our many long talks over cups of coffee

Coordinating editor: Ellen Rodger
Series editor: Carrie Gleason
Editors: Rachel Eagen, L. Michelle Nielsen
Design and production coordinator: Rosie Gowsell
Production assistance and book layout: Samara Parent
Art direction: Rob MacGregor
Photo research: Allison Napier

Photo Credits: Dbimages/Alamy: p. 1; Danita Delimont/Alamy: p. 21 (top), p. 25 (top); Holt Studios International Ltd./Alamy: cover; Mary Evans Picture Library/Alamy: p. 18 (bottom); The Art Archive/Bibliothèque des Arts Décoratifs Paris/Dagli Orti: p. 12; The Art Archive/Dagli Orti: p. 28 (top); The Art Archive/Private Collection/Dagli Orti: p. 22 (top); Art Resource, NY: p. 15 (bottom); Bildarchiv Preussischer Kulturbesitz/Art Resource, NY: p. 17 (bottom left); Bridgeman-Giraudon/Art Resource, NY: p. 5 (top); Werner Forman/Art Resource, NY: p. 11; AP/Wide World Photos: p. 27 (bottom), p. 30, p. 31; Bibliotheque des Arts Decoratifs, Paris, France, Archives Charmet/The Bridgeman Art Library: p. 10 (top); Private Collection, Bonhams, London, UK/The Bridgeman Art Library: p. 23; Blue Lantern Studio/Corbis: p. 22 (bottom); Jon Hicks/Corbis: p. 29 (top); Jeremy Horner/Corbis: p. 24, p. 26; Wolfgang Kaehler/Corbis: p. 16 (bottom); Earl & Nazima Kowall/Corbis: p. 4; Enzo & Paolo Ragazzini/Corbis: p. 7; Stapleton Collection/Corbis: p. 16 (top); Bruce Bennett Studios/Getty Images: p. 29 (bottom); The Granger Collection, New York: p. 9 (bottom), p. 19 (top); The British Museum/Topham-HIP/The Image Works: p. 10 (bottom); Mary Evans Picture Library/The Image Works: p. 13, p. 14, p. 21 (bottom); North Wind/North Wind Picture Archives: p. 20; Mark De Fraeye/Photo Researchers, Inc.: p. 8; Carl Frank/Photo Researchers, Inc.: p. 9 (top); Adam Hart-Davis/Photo Researchers, Inc.: p. 18 (middle); Jacana/Photo Researchers, Inc.: p. 25 (bottom); Sheila Terry/Photo Researchers, Inc.: p. 6 (top). Other images from stock CD.

Cartography: Jim Chernishenko: p. 6

Cover: A woman in Tanzania, in eastern Africa, harvests coffee berries. About 25 million farming families work on coffee plantations and farms around the world.

Title page: An Ethiopian woman sells coffee seeds, or beans, in a market. The coffee plant is believed to have originated, or first come from, Ethiopia, a country in northeast Africa. Coffee plants still grow wild in many countries in Africa, including the Ivory Coast, Zaire, and Uganda.

Contents page: It takes about 4,000 seeds to make only one pound (454 grams) of coffee.

Library and Archives Canada Cataloguing in Publication

Morganelli, Adrianna, 1979-
   The biography of coffee / Adrianna Morganelli.

(How did that get here?)
Includes index.
ISBN-13: 978-0-7787-2488-9 (bound)
ISBN-10: 0-7787-2488-3 (bound)
ISBN-13: 978-0-7787-2524-4 (pbk)
ISBN-10: 0-7787-2524-3 (pbk)

   1. Coffee--Juvenile literature. I. Title. II. Series.

SB269.M67 2006   j641.3'373   C2006-902467-7

Library of Congress Cataloging-in-Publication Data

Morganelli, Adrianna, 1979-
   The biography of coffee / written by Adrianna Morganelli.
      p. cm. -- (How did that get here?)
   Includes index.
   ISBN-13: 978-0-7787-2488-9 (rlb)
   ISBN-10: 0-7787-2488-3 (rlb)
   ISBN-13: 978-0-7787-2524-4 (pbk)
   ISBN-10: 0-7787-2524-3 (pbk)
   1. Coffee--Juvenile literature. I. Title. II. Series.
SB269.M855 2006
633.7'3--dc22
                                                2006014371

Crabtree Publishing Company

www.crabtreebooks.com   1-800-387-7650

Published in Canada
Crabtree Publishing
616 Welland Ave.
St. Catharines, ON
L2M 5V6

Published in the United States
Crabtree Publishing
PMB16A
350 Fifth Ave., Suite 3308
New York, NY 10118

Published in the United Kingdom
Crabtree Publishing
White Cross Mills
High Town, Lancaster
LA1 4XS

Published in Australia
Crabtree Publishing
386 Mt. Alexander Rd.
Ascot Vale (Melbourne)
VIC 3032

Contents

Coffee's Appeal

Coffee is the world's second most traded commodity, after oil. Commodities are goods that are bought and sold on world markets. Coffee is a dark, bitter beverage made from the roasted seeds, or beans, of the coffee plant. The coffee plant first grew in Ethiopia, in northeast Africa, where the ancient **Abyssinians** harvested the seeds and ate them. Later, the Abyssinians ground the seeds to make a beverage. Through trade, the **cultivation** of the coffee plant spread to other **tropical** countries, while the beverage became desired around the world. Today, coffee is also used to flavor liquor and desserts, such as cakes, ice creams, and sauces.

Coffee Around the World

Coffee is prepared in many different ways around the world. In North America, it is drunk black, or without anything added to it, or is flavored with cream, sugar, and sometimes with spices and honey. People in Belgium drink coffee from large bowls with big lumps of sugar, and dunk thick pieces of buttered bread into the mixture. In Brazil, people drink coffee from cups filled with sugar and equal amounts of coffee and milk, called *café com leite*, in the morning. In the afternoon, Brazilians drink *cafezinho*, which is coffee mixed in a pan with boiled water and sugar. It is drunk from tiny cups. In El Salvador, coffee is flavored with cinnamon, cloves, allspice, cardamom, and cloves, and is often drunk chilled over crushed ice.

(right) An Ethiopian woman uses a long pole to grind coffee the traditional way.

4

Coffee Houses

Restaurants called coffee houses or cafés specialize in serving coffee. They also serve tea, desserts, and sandwiches, and some offer alcoholic beverages or hot meals. Throughout their history, coffee houses have served as places where people met to discuss local and world issues, write and read literature, and play games. Insurance companies, **literary magazines**, and important changes in art and culture have all begun in coffee houses. Today's coffee houses, or coffee shops, are still places where people go to socialize, and many have grown over time into big businesses.

(right) A poster advertising a Paris café in the 1920s. Cafés are popular places for people to meet.

▼ *Roasted coffee beans, or seeds, are used to make coffee.*

ÉVITER LES CONTREFAÇONS

CAFÉ MARTIN
EUGÈNE MARTIN 33, Rue Joubert - PARIS

A Quick Pick Me Up

Coffee makes people feel less drowsy and more alert because it contains a chemical called caffeine. Consuming too much caffeine can cause a person to feel nervous, or have difficulty falling asleep. The flavor of coffee and the caffeine's **stimulating** effects have made coffee one of the world's most popular beverages for adults.

▸ *Many adults around the world drink coffee to give them an energy boost.*

Coffee Country

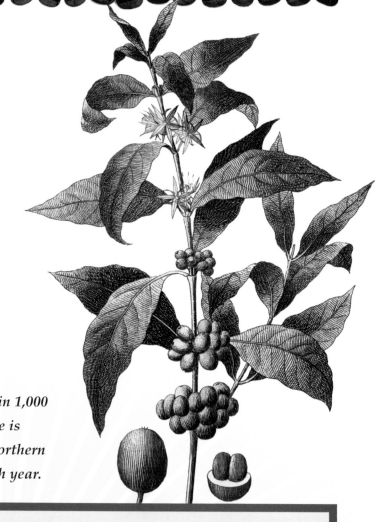

Coffee first grew wild in Africa. Today, because of the high demand for coffee, it is cultivated in more than 65 countries around the world. The coffee plant is grown in South and Central America, Africa, Asia, and the Caribbean Islands. More than half of the world's coffee is cultivated on small farms with only a few acres. Many coffee plants are also grown on large farms called plantations that employ hundreds of laborers, or workers.

▶ *Coffee is made from the seeds of the coffee plant. The seeds have to be removed from inside the red coffee berry.*

(below) Coffee plants are grown in countries within 1,000 miles (1,609 kilometers) of the equator. Most coffee is consumed far from where it is grown, such as in northern Europe, where people consume the most coffee each year.

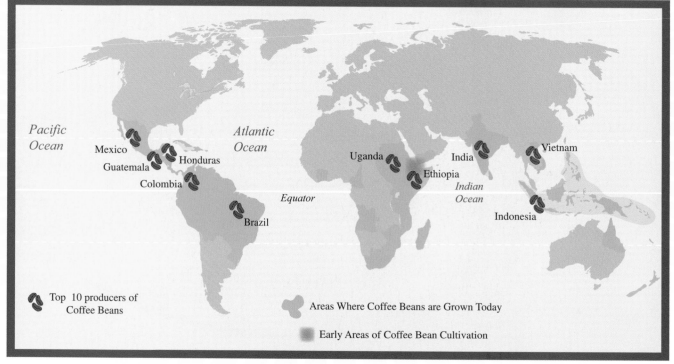

Pacific Ocean

Atlantic Ocean

Mexico
Guatemala
Honduras
Colombia
Brazil
Equator

Uganda
Ethiopia
India
Vietnam
Indian Ocean
Indonesia

🫘 Top 10 producers of Coffee Beans

Areas Where Coffee Beans are Grown Today

Early Areas of Coffee Bean Cultivation

Growing Different Kinds of Coffee

There are about 60 different species, or types, of coffee plants. The two main types grown for export are *coffea arabica* and *coffea robusta*. Today, 80 percent of the world's coffee comes from the *coffea arabica* plant. *Coffea arabica* originated in Ethiopia, and it still grows wild in the country's mountainous rainforests. It is also now grown throughout Indonesia, East Africa, and South America. In the late 1800s, another type of coffee plant called *coffea robusta* was discovered growing wild in the Congo, in central Africa. *Coffea robusta* now grows in West Africa, Southeast Asia, and Indonesia, and accounts for 20 percent of the world's coffee. *Coffea robusta* produces more than twice as many seeds as the *arabica* type, is less **vulnerable** to disease, and is easier to grow. The *robusta* seeds have a bitter flavor and are mixed with *arabica* seeds to produce better tasting coffee.

Top Coffee Producers

About 27 million acres (11 million hectares) of coffee is cultivated around the world. Brazil is the top producer, supplying about 30 percent of the world's coffee. About 85 percent of Brazil's plantations grow *coffea arabica*. Brazil is also the second largest producer of *coffea robusta*. Colombia, Mexico, Ethiopia, and Guatemala also produce a lot of the world's *coffea arabica*. Vietnam produces the most *coffea robusta* in the world. Other countries that produce a lot of *coffea robusta* are Indonesia, India, and Uganda. The countries that make up South and Central America produce about two-thirds of the world's total coffee supply.

(below) Coffee plants growing on mountainsides on a Colombian plantation.

The Coffee Plant

The coffee plant is an **evergreen** shrub that grows in tropical countries where sunshine and rainfall are plentiful and temperatures are warm. Coffee plants thrive when they are shaded from direct sunlight. They grow best in temperatures ranging from 59°F to 77°F (15°C to 25°C), in rich, fertile soil. Wild coffee plants grow more than 20 feet (six meters) tall and live for up to 60 years. After about four years, coffee plants produce clusters of white blossoms. The blossoms have a sweet scent to attract insects, which **pollinate** the plants' blossoms to produce berries. The blossoms remain on the coffee plants for a few days, and are replaced with small green coffee berries.

The Coffee Cherry

It takes between six to nine months for coffee berries to ripen. The green berries turn deep red, or yellow, in some varieties of the plant. Ripe coffee berries are called "cherries" because they are the same size and color as a cherry. Underneath the berry's red skin is a soft, fleshy, sweet substance called pulp. Inside the pulp are two seeds, which are coated with a husk, or thin yellow shell called silver skin. The silver skin is peeled off to reveal the seeds, which vary in color and size according to the species of the coffee plant. Most coffee seeds are tiny and bluish green or yellow.

(left) One branch of a coffee plant can have blossoms, and unripe, ripe, and overripe berries growing at the same time.

(above) On coffee plantations, farmers inspect their crop. Heavy winds, hail, and too much or too little rain can damage an entire coffee crop.

(below, right) Some coffee seeds are stripped of their caffeine to make decaffeinated coffee.

Growing on Plantations

Coffee plants are grown in greenhouses until they are a few inches tall. After about six months, they are **transplanted** into rows about three to ten feet (one to three meters) apart on a coffee plantation. On some plantations, farmers plant fruit trees between the rows to protect the coffee plants from high winds and too much sunlight. Most coffee comes from sun plantations, where coffee is grown without the shade of other trees. Sun plantations are located high on mountain slopes where the coffee plants are shaded by clouds. The plants are regularly **pruned** to about 12 to 15 feet (four to five meters) high to make harvesting easier. During the growing season, farmers inspect coffee plants for diseases, such as leaf rust, and for insects that damage the crops. In some types of coffee plants, the first crop is ready to be harvested three to five years after planting. Coffee plants continue to bear berries for ten to 25 years. When the plants no longer produce suitable berries, farmers prune them back so that only the branches that produce the best fruit survive.

Caffeine Kills Pests

The leaves and berries of the coffee plant contain an **addictive** chemical called caffeine. Caffeine is also found in other plants, such as the tea bush, and the cacao plant, from which chocolate is made. In plants, caffeine works as a natural pesticide, or chemical that kills the insects that feed on them. The amount of caffeine in coffee varies depending on the type of coffee plant they came from, and the way the seeds are roasted. Drinking coffee that contains caffeine makes people feel more mentally and physically alert, and increases body coordination. Consuming too much caffeine makes people feel restless, dizzy, and causes headaches.

Drink this hearty coffee as strong as you like...

It still can't get on your nerves! Drink as many cups as you like... as often as you like... Sanka still can't make you jittery or keep you awake. All pure coffee. 97% caffein-free.

NEW INSTANT SANKA COFFEE

Coffee's First Cultivators

Scientists believe that the coffee plant originally grew wild in the mountains of ancient Abyssinia, which is present-day Ethiopia. Around 850 A.D., the Abyssinians first ate the leaves and berries of the coffee plant. They ground the seeds of the coffee berry, mixed the grounds with animal fat or butter, and formed the mixture into balls, which they ate before battle for energy. Over time, they made a beverage with crushed coffee seeds by brewing them with boiled water. They then **fermented** the sweet pulp of the berries to make wine.

▸ *From Africa, coffee spread to Arabia, or the southwestern part of the Arabian peninsula.*

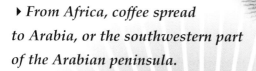

The Ethiopian Legend of Kaldi

According to legend, around 850 A.D., an Abyssinian goat herder named Kaldi discovered his goats leaping and bleating wildly after eating the leaves and berries of a coffee plant. Kaldi tried the leaves and berries for himself, and found that he too suddenly felt excited, clear headed, and happy. He showed the berries to the monks, or holy men, at a nearby **monastery**. The monks were skeptical of the berries' power and threw them into a fire. As the berries roasted, a rich aroma filled the monastery, and the monks raked them from the fire and put out the flames. They soaked the roasted berries in a pitcher of hot water and drank the new beverage. This was the first cup of coffee.

◂ **Qishr** *is another early beverage made from the coffee plant. The husks are boiled and served in bowls such as these.*

Arabia

Coffee plants were among the trade goods that crossed the Red Sea from Africa to Arabia. Historians believe that around 1000 A.D., Arabs began making coffee. Coffee was called *qahwa*, which means "wine" in Arabic, because its effect on people was similar to **intoxication** caused by alcohol. Drinking alcohol was forbidden in **Islam**, the religion followed by most Arabs. Religious leaders could not come to an agreement on whether or not coffee should also be banned. Despite being advised against drinking coffee, many Arabs continued to drink it. By the late 1400s, Arabs had traded coffee seeds with the people of North Africa, Persia, or present-day Iran, Egypt, and Turkey.

Control of the Coffee Trade

Only seeds that had been boiled or partially roasted were exported by Arab traders. This ensured that the seeds would not grow into coffee plants if they were planted in other countries. Arab control of the coffee trade ended in 1536, when the **Ottoman Turks** invaded Yemen, in Arabia. They took control of the coffee trade, and traded coffee throughout their empire, which included areas of the **Middle East** and Europe, which made them very wealthy.

(above) According to legend, seven fertile coffee seeds from Arabia were smuggled to India and planted on the mountainsides of southern India, where the coffee plants flourished.

Coffee Spreads

From the early 1400s to the 1600s, European countries sent ships of exploration in search of trade routes to Asia. Countries such as Spain, France, England, and the Netherlands, explored lands they did not know before, such as Asia, the Americas, and Africa, where they built **colonies**. Europeans raided these lands for their resources and traded them with other countries, making Europeans very wealthy. They found new crops in Asia, Africa, and the Americas, and introduced others, including coffee plants, to their colonies.

▼ *A Turkish woman is served coffee by a servant.*

Dutch Control

The Ottoman Turks **monopolized** the coffee trade until 1616, when Dutch explorers from the Netherlands smuggled coffee berries from Arabia. The Dutch planted coffee in their colony on the island of Ceylon, or present-day Sri Lanka. By 1700, the Dutch had also transplanted coffee seeds to their colonies in Indonesia. There were not enough coffee plants being cultivated in Dutch colonies to meet the rising demand for coffee in Europe, which caused the price of coffee to be so high that only very wealthy Europeans could afford to drink it.

The French Caribbean

In 1669, a Turkish **ambassador** to France introduced coffee to the French. The French found the beverage too bitter, and added sugar to sweeten it. Coffee sweetened with sugar soon became very popular in Europe, and people also began to add cream to the beverage. In 1713, the Dutch gave coffee plants as gifts to France's king. Gabriel Mathieu de Clieu, a French navy officer, visited Paris from the French colony of Martinique, in the Caribbean. He asked the king for coffee plants so that he could grow coffee in Martinique. De Clieu's request was granted, and he sailed back to Martinique with two young coffee plants. Only one plant survived the journey, which he planted in his own garden. About two years later, the plant **yielded** about two pounds (0.9 kilograms) of coffee berries, which were shipped to other French colonies in the Caribbean to be cultivated.

Coffee Cultivation in Brazil

The Portuguese wanted to grow coffee plants in their colony in Brazil, but did not have seeds. In 1727, a Brazilian named Francisco de Melho Palheta went to the French-controlled region of Guiana, in northern South America, to ask the French governor for some coffee seeds. The French governor refused. The governor's wife, unable to resist de Melho Palheta's charms, secretly slipped some coffee berries into his hand before he returned to Brazil. The seeds of the berries were planted in Para, in Brazil, and soon coffee cultivation spread throughout the rest of the country. By the early 1800s, Brazil's coffee cultivation flourished, and the country prospered from trading coffee with the countries of Europe and North, Central, and South America.

British Cultivation

By 1877, British colonists planted thousands of acres of coffee on plantations in their colonies in India and Ceylon. They used the people who lived there to harvest the crops, which yielded about one million pounds (454,000 kilograms) of coffee each year. When a plant disease destroyed the coffee plantations in India and Ceylon, British colonists planted coffee seeds in their colonies in Kenya and Uganda, in East Africa. In 1898, the British discovered *coffea robusta* growing wild in the Congo, and transported the coffee plants to their African colonies.

(above) When fresh water on de Clieu's ship began to run out, he shared his own water with the young coffee plants to keep them alive.

Slavery on Coffee Plantations

Many laborers were needed to work on coffee plantations in Europe's colonies overseas. Plantation owners often used local people as slaves to harvest and process coffee because more profit could be made by not paying them. Men were forced to do physically demanding work, such as clearing land, planting and pruning coffee plants, and digging **irrigation** ditches. Women and children mostly harvested the plants and sorted the coffee seeds. Many slaves died from overwork and European diseases, such as influenza.

(above) In the 1880s, Dutch planters in Java and Sumatra, in Indonesia, forced native families to grow and harvest coffee plants.

Slavery in Brazil

In the early 1800s, thousands of African slaves worked on coffee plantations, called *fazendas*, in Brazil. The slaves were forced to work about 17 hours a day for no pay, and were given only one meal. They had no personal possessions, and were beaten as punishment when coffee plantation owners, called coffee barons, felt that they did not harvest enough coffee. Coffee barons were very wealthy and lived on plantations in large houses with servants. They were armed with guns at all times, in case slaves rebelled, or rose up against them. By 1828, there were more than one million slaves working on plantations in Brazil, including coffee and sugar cane plantations.

The Colonos System

Immigrants from Europe, called *colonos*, were also brought to Brazil to work on coffee plantations. Most of the immigrants were from Italy, but many also came from Portugal, Spain, and Germany. The *colonos* were indentured laborers, which means that they were bound by contract to work for the coffee barons for a specific period of time. The coffee barons paid for their passage to Brazil, and gave them houses and land so they could grow their own food. It was illegal for the *colonos* to leave the plantation until they paid off their debts to the coffee barons for their living arrangements. The *colonos* were not well paid, which made it difficult for them to repay their debts. In 1884, the Brazilian government agreed to pay for their passage to Brazil, and many more European immigrants arrived to work on the plantations.

▲ *In 1901, more than 16 million bags of coffee seeds were exported from coffee plantations in Sao Paolo, in southeastern Brazil. Today, Brazil is the top producer of* **coffea arabica.**

(above) In the early 1900s, more than 500 million coffee plants were grown on Sao Paolo plantations by European immigrants called **colonos.**

Early Coffee Houses

During the 1400s, the first coffee houses, called *kaveh kanes*, opened throughout Arabia, where people went to drink coffee, socialize, gamble, and play games such as backgammon and chess. As coffee houses grew in popularity, many Arab leaders began to worry that the people gathering there were discussing the wrongdoings of their leaders. Many Muslims also believed that drinking coffee went against Islamic teachings and that it should be forbidden. In 1511, the governor of Mecca, in present-day Saudi Arabia, ordered that all coffee houses be closed. People continued to drink coffee and coffee houses continued to be opened.

(above) Coffee houses in Turkey admitted only men. In addition to drinking coffee, coffee houses were also a place where men went to smoke.

▼ *An Arab coffee pot, or dallah.*

Turkey

Turkey was the center of the Ottoman empire. Its first coffee house was opened in the capital city of Constantinople, or present-day Istanbul, in 1554. The Grand Vizier of Constantinople, a high level government official, closed the city's coffee houses because he feared that the conversation in coffee houses would lead to rebellion. People continued to drink coffee in secret because they enjoyed the increase in energy that coffee created. Anyone found drinking coffee was first beaten with a stick. They were sewn into a leather bag and thrown in the river if found drinking coffee again.

Europe

Europe's first shipment of coffee seeds arrived in the port of Venice, Italy, in 1615. The **Catholic priests** of Europe believed that coffee was **unholy**, and asked the leader of the Catholic Church, the Pope, to ban it. It is believed that when the Pope tasted coffee, he liked it so much that he refused to ban it. Coffee became a luxury item in Europe, and was only drunk by the wealthy. By the 1650s, coffee was sold on streets in Italy by *aquacedratajo*, or lemonade vendors, who also sold chocolate and alcohol. Venice's first coffee house, called a *caffe*, opened in 1683. Coffee houses only admitted men and served food as well as coffee.

◄ *A German coffee vendor from the 1700s.*

▶ *The custom of tipping waiters and waitresses began in English coffee houses. People who wanted good service and the best seats in the house put money inside a tin jar labeled "To Insure Prompt Services."*

England's Penny Universities

In 1652, London's first coffee house was established. The owner attracted customers by claiming that coffee aided **digestion**, and cured headaches and diseases. The coffee house was an immediate success, and other coffee houses sprang up throughout the country. England's king was against coffee houses because he felt they were **immoral** and provoked negative political discussion. The king banned England's coffee houses, but was forced to reopen them only 11 days later due to the uproar. By the late 1700s, there were more than 2,000 coffee houses in London, and thousands more throughout England. England's coffee houses were called penny universities, because a cup of coffee cost one penny, and conversations about world issues educated listeners.

France's Artful Houses

In France, coffee houses were called cafés. The first café opened in Marseilles, France, in 1670. Many doctors in France declared that drinking coffee was harmful to people's health, and caused **paralysis** and exhaustion. Other doctors defended coffee, and prescribed the drink to patients suffering from problems with their bowels and skin. When cafés opened in Paris, actors, authors, and musicians met at them to discuss the arts and drink coffee and other beverages.

◄ *In 1674, women in England signed a petition to close down coffee houses because they felt men were spending too much time away from their homes and families to socialize in coffee houses (below).*

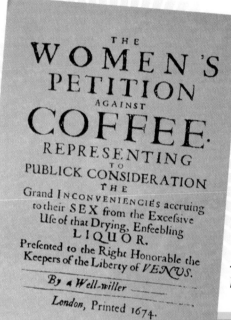

THE WOMEN'S PETITION AGAINST COFFEE. REPRESENTING TO PUBLICK CONSIDERATION THE Grand INCONVENIENCIES accruing to their SEX from the Excessive Use of that Drying, Enfeebling LIQUOR.

Presented to the Right Honorable the Keepers of the Liberty of VENUS.

By a Well-willer

London, Printed 1674.

Vienna's Victory

In 1683, the Ottoman Turks sailed to Vienna, in Austria, to conquer the land, and were defeated. The Turks fled Vienna, leaving behind their supplies, which included 500 sacks of coffee seeds. The Viennese had never seen coffee seeds before, and thought the seeds were feed for the Turks' camels. They began to burn the sacks, and a rich aroma was released. A Viennese man, who had once lived in Arabia, recognized the aroma and knew that they were burning coffee. He took the seeds and opened the first coffee house in Austria, called the Blue Bottle. Coffee houses became very popular in Vienna, and were soon established throughout Austria.

▲ *To celebrate the Austrian victory over the Ottoman Turks, bakers created pastries in the shape of crescent moons, which was the symbol of Islam. These pastries are known as croissants.*

Coffee in America

Until the late 1700s, tea was the most popular drink in North America. Tea was supplied to the American colonists by the British. In 1765, England's King George III imposed a high tax on all goods, including tea, that were imported, or sold to, the colonies. On December 16, 1773, a group of about 50 men boarded English ships in Boston Harbor, and emptied the tea from 343 chests into the water. This event became known as the Boston Tea Party. It became a patriotic duty not to drink tea, and coffee houses were established throughout America.

(right) When England's King George heard that the American colonists had dumped the tea into the harbor he is rumored to have said "Let them drink coffee."

Coffee Making Innovations

During the 1800s, the demand for coffee grew in North America. People enjoyed drinking coffee in coffee houses throughout the country, and many people brewed coffee in their homes. Consumers bought raw, or green, coffee seeds at general stores, and roasted, ground, and brewed the coffee themselves.

▼ *During the American Civil War, soldiers were given a daily ration of coffee to help them stay alert. They carried whole coffee seeds with them and ground them when needed before brewing them over campfires.*

In the Early Days

The most popular method of roasting coffee seeds in the early 1800s was in a frying pan on a wood stove. Coffee seeds are roasted to fully develop the rich flavor and aroma of coffee. Roasting required about 20 minutes of constant stirring, and often produced seeds that were raw inside and burnt on the outside. Some people roasted their seeds inside small machines in which the seeds were turned by a crank so that they roasted evenly.

Roasting Innovations

By the mid-1840s, a coffee roasting industry developed in the United States. Many inventors received **patents** for coffee roasters. The most popular roaster at the time was the Carter Pull-Out Roaster, invented in 1846 by Bostonian James W. Carter. The roaster featured large cylinders with holes in them, which rotated inside brick ovens. Coffee seeds were placed inside the cylinders to roast, and when fully roasted, workers pulled the cylinders out of the machine and dumped the seeds into wooden trays, where they were stirred with shovels to cool down. In 1864, Jabez Burns invented a self-emptying roaster. Inside the roaster, the coffee seeds were roasted as they were pushed up and down a chamber as the cylinder turned. When the door of the roaster was opened, the roasted seeds tumbled out onto a cooling tray. Burns sold hundreds of roasters in the United States.

(above) Today, coffee seeds are roasted in large metal machines called drum roasters, and dumped into cooling bins.

▼ *More coffee companies were established after roasting machines were invented. Using catchy advertisements, the companies competed against one another for customers.*

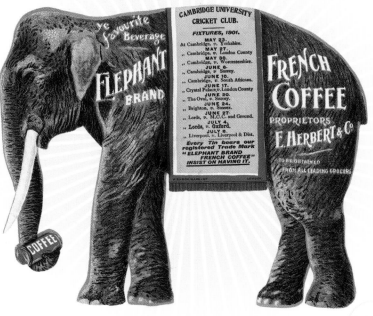

Grinding

During the 1800s, roasted coffee seeds were ground at a mill, or by hand with a mortar and pestle. Today, coffee seeds are ground in factories after roasting. The seeds travel through a series of cylinders, which turn in opposite directions to break them into tiny pieces. The ground coffee is packaged in airtight containers to keep it fresh, and sold to stores. Some consumers prefer to grind their own seeds, rather than purchase seeds that have been ground at a factory. Many people use electric grinders at home, which are small appliances run by electric motors that grind the seeds within seconds.

▼ *Hand turned coffee mills were used in the past for grinding coffee at home.*

Brewing

The flavor, aroma, and color of coffee are released when the ground seeds are brewed with hot water. The fineness of the ground seeds and the brewing method affects the flavor of the coffee. Seeds that are too finely ground produce strong, bitter tasting coffee, and coffee made from overly coarse seeds is watery and lacks flavor. In the early 1800s, people brewed coffee by boiling the grounds in water. Eggshells, dried eel skins, or other fish were added to the brew to help settle the grounds to the bottom of the cup. This affected the taste of the coffee.

(left) Trade cards were advertisements that came in packages of coffee. The cards showed different pictures and people collected them.

Brewing Innovations

In the early 1800s, Jean Baptiste de Belloy, from France, invented the drip pot, which was used to brew coffee. Ground coffee seeds were placed inside an upper compartment and hot water was poured over them. The water slowly dripped through a filter made from a metal disk that had holes in it and into a bottom compartment. A coffee maker called a percolator was invented in France in 1827. The percolator was designed to heat water and brew coffee in one operation, by pumping hot water through coffee grounds. This brewing method is convenient and easy, and is still used around the world today. Most people today use drip brew coffee makers, which were introduced in the 1970s. The machine boils water, which drips onto the coffee grounds inside a filter made of paper or metal with small holes. The filtered coffee then drips into a coffee pot.

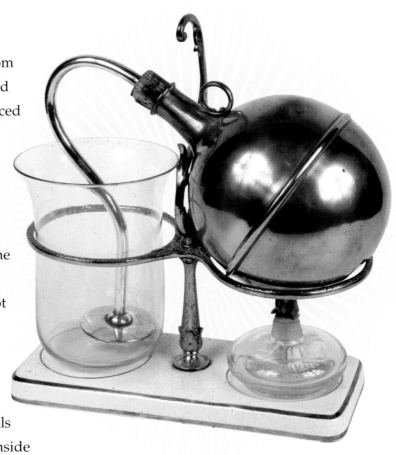

▲ *The Napier vacuum coffee maker was invented in the 1840s.*

▲ *Modern-day coffee makers still use paper filters.*

Melitta's Filtered Coffee

Filtered coffee was invented by a German housewife named Melitta Bentz in 1908. At the time, people put ground coffee seeds into cloth bags and brewed them in hot water. Often, the grounds seeped into the coffee when the bags became worn, making the beverage undesirable to drink. The strength of new bags also made it difficult to extract flavor from the seeds. Bentz placed a sheet of **blotting paper** inside a brass pot that had holes in the bottom, and poured hot water through the top. She discovered that the grounds remained inside the paper, and did not seep into the beverage. The first year, Bentz sold 1,250 coffee filters at a fair. By 1912, she had established a business to manufacture coffee filters. Today, the Melitta company still sells coffee filters as well as coffee and coffee makers.

From Field to Cup

The quality of coffee depends on the ripeness of the berries, so picking coffee berries is an important stage of harvesting coffee. Growers test the berries for ripeness by squeezing them with their fingers. The berry is ripe when the seeds easily squirt out from the skin.

Harvesting the Berries

On some large coffee plantations, machines are used to pick the berries. When coffee is mechanically harvested, both ripe and unripe berries are picked, so many berries are wasted, and there is a risk that the unripe berries will spoil the taste of the coffee. The harvested berries are immersed in water to sort the ripe berries from the unripe ones. When placed in water, the ripe berries sink, and the unripe berries float. On most plantations, the ripe berries are picked by hand by laborers who are paid for each basket of berries that they collect. The unripe berries are left on the plants to be harvested when they are ripe.

▶ *An experienced laborer can collect six to seven baskets of coffee berries in one day, but they are paid very little for each basket of berries they collect.*

Getting at the Seeds

There are many methods to remove the seeds from the coffee berry, and each method produces a different flavor of coffee. Most of the world's coffee berries are processed using the wet method. In the wet method, coffee berries are soaked overnight in a tank of water to soften them. A machine called a pulpier presses the coffee berries against a screen with holes large enough for only the seeds to pass through. The ripe berries break apart against the screen, removing the skin and some of the pulp, and the seeds are released. The coffee seeds are then left to ferment in tanks for several days, after which they·are flushed with water to remove the remaining pulp. The seeds are spread outdoors to be dried by the sun. When the air is moist, or humid, the seeds are dried by machines to prevent mildew from forming. Once dry, the husks surrounding the seeds are removed by machines.

(above) Coffee berries can also be pulped by hand.

Kopi Luwak

Kopi Luwak is a specialty coffee sold mainly in Japan that is made in Southern India, Asia, and Indonesia. It is made from coffee seeds that have passed through the digestive system of a cat-like animal called the palm civet. The animal climbs coffee plants and eats the berries, and excretes the seeds in its waste because it cannot digest them. The coffee seeds are then gathered by local farmers and made into coffee. Kopi Luwak is the most expensive coffee in the world, costing about $300 for only one pound (454 grams) of coffee.

▼ *The palm civet eats coffee berries.*

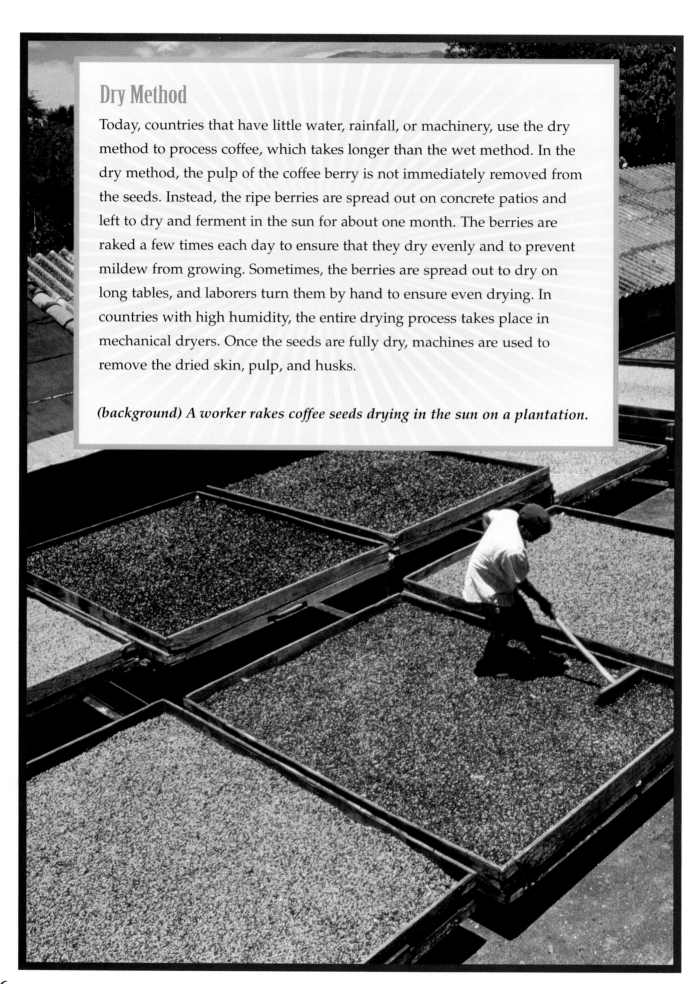

Dry Method

Today, countries that have little water, rainfall, or machinery, use the dry method to process coffee, which takes longer than the wet method. In the dry method, the pulp of the coffee berry is not immediately removed from the seeds. Instead, the ripe berries are spread out on concrete patios and left to dry and ferment in the sun for about one month. The berries are raked a few times each day to ensure that they dry evenly and to prevent mildew from growing. Sometimes, the berries are spread out to dry on long tables, and laborers turn them by hand to ensure even drying. In countries with high humidity, the entire drying process takes place in mechanical dryers. Once the seeds are fully dry, machines are used to remove the dried skin, pulp, and husks.

(background) A worker rakes coffee seeds drying in the sun on a plantation.

Sorting and Grading

Dry coffee seeds are sorted and graded by size, shape, and color. Debris, such as twigs and stones, and seeds that are rotten, discolored, or damaged, are removed. In some countries, seeds are sorted by hand. In other countries, seeds are sorted using machines. The coffee seeds are stored in burlap sacks, and are kept dry and cool. The weight of a sack of seeds varies in each country, but the most common weight of each is 132 pounds (60 kilograms). Before the coffee is sold, the seeds are inspected. Professional tasters, called cuppers, gather samples of seeds, and roast, grind, and brew them to make them into coffee. After the samples have been tasted, the bags are graded and exported.

Selling Coffee

Coffee seeds pass through many hands before they reach the consumer. Coffee dealers purchase coffee seeds from farmers and sell them to coffee suppliers. The dealers sell the seeds for a profit at the Coffee, Sugar, and Cocoa Exchange, which is where coffee and other commodities are traded. Coffee suppliers roast the seeds and package them before selling them to buyers, which are companies that sell coffee to consumers. Each time the coffee seeds are resold, the price is raised so that the seller makes a profit. The price of the seeds rises when there is a high demand for coffee, or when coffee production decreases due to plant diseases or severe weather conditions, such as drought or frost. When farmers harvest more coffee than consumers can buy, the price of the seeds drops.

(above) It takes about 600,000 coffee seeds to fill one burlap sack.

(left) Cuppers are professional coffee tasters.

27

The Business of Coffee

Today, about one and a half billion cups of coffee are consumed around the world every day. People buy coffee at coffee houses, restaurants, and food stores. Many companies sell ground coffee in sealed containers in food stores around the world.

The Big Four

The prices that coffee farmers are paid for their seeds depends on how much money large companies are willing to pay for the coffee. Today, large multinational companies that buy and sell coffee include Procter and Gamble, Sara Lee, Kraft Foods, and Nestlé. Multinational companies operate in more than one country and manufacture many consumer goods.

(right) In the early 1900s, when too much coffee was produced, it was thrown over the sides of ships to keep prices from falling.

Folger's Black Gold

In 1850, Edward, Henry, and James Folger, three brothers from Nantucket, Massachusetts, set sail for California to seek their fortunes in the gold rush. James Folger found work in San Francisco at a coffee and spice mill, where he discovered that many gold miners did not have equipment to roast and grind their own coffee seeds. Folger roasted and ground the coffee seeds, and sold them to the miners. By the end of the 1870s, Folgers was supplying coffee to people throughout the United States. Today, Folgers coffee is one of the best known coffee brands in North America.

(above) Many small, independent coffee shops have closed down due to the large number of people that visit coffee shop chains.

Coffee Chains

Today, there are large coffee shop chains where people purchase brewed coffee. A chain is a type of business where all stores are under one main ownership or where individual owners buy a store and run it like all the others. Starbucks Coffee Company, founded in 1971 in Seattle, Washington, is the largest chain of coffee shops in the world today. Thousands of Starbucks coffee shops around the world sell specialty coffees and coffee making equipment. Tim Hortons is the largest chain of coffee shops in Canada. The first Tim Hortons was opened in 1964 in Hamilton, Ontario. Today, there are more than 2,600 Tim Hortons shops across Canada, where coffee, donuts, soups, and sandwiches are also sold.

▲ Canada's largest coffee shop chain is named after National Hockey League (NHL) player Tim Horton.

Fair Trade Coffee

Most of the world's coffee is grown on small farms, where coffee-farming families are paid little for their seeds. On coffee plantations, laborers are paid low wages, and many cannot afford to pay for food, shelter, education, or health care. Some laborers bring their children to the fields to help them harvest their daily **quota** of coffee. Some consumers refuse to purchase coffee from plantations and farms where laborers are not paid fairly. Instead, they purchase coffee supported by fair trade, which is a movement that ensures laborers receive fair wages. Fair trade guarantees consumers that coffee was cultivated in safe and healthy working conditions.

Saving Rainforests

Fair trade coffee also supports coffee harvesting practices that do not harm the environment. In many coffee producing countries, rainforests are burned or cut down to make room for coffee plantations. The destruction of the rainforests leaves wildlife, such as birds, insects, butterflies, and other animals, without a habitat, or home. Today, in many countries, such as Brazil, some farmers protect the environment and conserve animal habitats by planting coffee in existing forests, where the trees are used to shade the growing coffee plants. Sometimes, other plants, such as banana and nut trees, are transplanted to coffee farms and plantations.

▶ *To promote fair trade coffee, a man dresses in a traditional Native Mexican costume at a fair. Hundreds of years ago, during the colonization of Central America, the lands of the Native peoples were taken from them and converted into coffee plantations.*

Organic Coffee

On many farms and plantations, chemical fertilizers and pesticides are sprayed on coffee plants while they grow. Pesticides are used to get rid of insects that harm the plants, and fertilizers are nutrients that are added to the soil to help plants grow. These chemicals pollute soil and water, which puts people at risk of drinking contaminated, or dirty, water. Fair trade coffee is cultivated on farms and plantations that harvest coffee organically. Organic coffee is fertilized with **composted** coffee pulp, which supplies the soil with nutrients. Animal manure is also used as fertilizer. The waste water from the fermentation tanks is used for irrigation, rather than dumped into lakes and rivers.

(background) A coffee farmer on a Costa Rican plantation sprays pesticides onto coffee plants to keep pests away.

Glossary

Abyssinians The name once given to the people of present-day Ethiopia

addictive A substance containing chemicals that causes users to become physically dependent, or feel they have to have it

ambassador A country's representative

blotting paper An absorbent paper that was placed over top of ink writing so that it would not smear

Catholic priests Men who lead religious ceremonies in the Catholic Church. The Catholic Church is a branch of Christianity

colony Land ruled by a distant country

compost Rotting organic, or once living, matter

cultivation The farming and harvesting of a crop

digestion The process in which a body breaks down food into nutrients

evergreen A plant that keeps its leaves all year

ferment To sour

immigrant A person who moves to another country

immoral Not caring about right and wrong

intoxication An altered state due to substance intake, usually too much alcohol

irrigation a system for watering crops

Islam A religion that believes in one god and follows the teachings of the prophet Muhammad

literary magazines magazines about writing

Middle East An area of land that extends from the eastern Mediterranean to the Persian Gulf

monastery The place where monks live

monopolize To have sole control over

Ottoman Turks (Empire) A group of Turkish-speaking people who established a large empire in Southeast Europe, the Middle East, and North Africa that lasted from the late 1200s to 1923

paralysis Not able to move

patent A license that identifies someone as the inventor of something

pollinate To move pollen from one plant to another for reproduction

prune To cut back branches on a tree or bush

quota A required amount

stimulating Something that excites the senses

transplant To plant seedlings, or young plants, somewhere else

tropical The warm regions of the world just north and south of the equator

unholy Not allowed by the Church

vulnerable At risk of being hurt

yield The amount of crop produced in a season

Index

Fossil Ridge Public Library District
Braidwood, IL 60408

Printed in the U.S.A.